HOW ARE LAWS MADE?

**We the People:
U.S. Government at Work**

Kevin Winn

Published in the United States of America by:

Cherry Lake Press
2395 South Huron Parkway, Suite 200, Ann Arbor, Michigan 48104
www.cherrylakepress.com

Reading Adviser: Beth Walker Gambro, MS, Ed., Reading Consultant, Yorkville, IL
Content Adviser: Mark Richards, Ph.D., Professor, Dept. of Political Science, Grand Valley State University, Allendale, MI

Photo Credits: cover: Pamela Au/Shutterstock; page 5: © Orhan Cam/Shutterstock; page 6: United States Senate; page 7: Collection of the U.S. House of Representatives; page 8: Education & Labor Committee/U.S. House of Representatives; page 9: Andrew Harnik/Associated Press, U.S. Senate Democrats; page 11: © Joe Tabb/ Dreamstime.com; page 12: U.S. Senate Committee on Health, Education, Labor & Pensions/U.S. Senate; page 14: Office of Dan Sullivan/U.S. Senate; page 16: © Trong Nguyen/Shutterstock; page 19: © 1000 Words/Shutterstock; page 20: © Prostock-studio/Shutterstock; page 21: © ESB Professional/Shutterstock

Copyright © 2023 by Cherry Lake Publishing Group

All rights reserved. No part of this book may be reproduced or utilized in any form or by any means without written permission from the publisher.

Cherry Lake Press is an imprint of Cherry Lake Publishing Group.

Library of Congress Cataloging-in-Publication Data

Names: Winn, Kevin P., author.
Title: How are laws made? / Kevin Winn.
Description: Ann Arbor, Michigan : Cherry Lake Publishing, [2023] | Series: We the people: U.S. government at work | Audience: Grades 2-3
Summary: "We the People: U.S. Government at Work explains the basic building blocks of U.S. democracy from detailing what democracy is to describing how the three branches of government work together. Young readers will also discover how they play a key role in American democracy. Series is aligned to 21st Century Skills curriculum standards. Engaging inquiry-based sidebars encourage students to Think, Create, Guess, and Ask Questions. Includes table of contents, glossary, index, author biography, and sidebars"— Provided by publisher.
Identifiers: LCCN 2022039300 | ISBN 9781668919392 (hardcover) | ISBN 9781668920411 (paperback) | ISBN 9781668921746 (ebook) | ISBN 9781668923078 (pdf)
Subjects: LCSH: Legislation—United States—Juvenile literature. | United States. Congress—Juvenile literature. | United States—Politics and government—Juvenile literature.
Classification: LCC JK1025 .W55 2023 | DDC 328.73—dc23/eng/20221021
LC record available at https://lccn.loc.gov/2022039300

Cherry Lake Press would like to acknowledge the work of the Partnership for 21st Century Learning, a Network of Battelle for Kids. Please visit http://www.battelleforkids.org/networks/p21 for more information.

Printed in the United States of America
Corporate Graphics

CONTENTS

Chapter 1: Who Can Make Laws?   4

Chapter 2: How Does a Bill Become a Law?   10

Chapter 3: The Local Level   17

   Activity   20
   Glossary   22
   Find Out More   23
   Index   24
   About the Author   24

WHO CAN MAKE LAWS?

The United States has many laws. But how are they made? And who makes them? The lawmaking process can be complicated, but it's important. It's one of the U.S. Congress's biggest jobs.

Congress is made up of two parts. These are the Senate and the House of Representatives. Each state has two senators and at least one

The U.S. Congress has 100 senators and 435 representatives.

5

representative. The more people who live in a state, the more representatives that state has.

Our government is made up of three branches. These are the executive, legislative, and judicial branches.

The Senate (left) and House (right) Chambers are where representatives meet to debate and vote on laws.

Create!

You have a voice. You can make change. Make a list of your representatives. Choose one and write to them about an idea for a law that you have.

Congress is part of the legislative branch. To **legislate** means to make or to put into practice. It's Congress's job to create laws.

Representatives must work together to make laws.

8

Ideas for laws can come from anyone. You don't need to be an **elected** official. But only elected officials may pass a national law. Many steps happen before an idea becomes a law.

HOW DOES A BILL BECOME A LAW?

Someone has an idea for a law. What happens next? There are many steps. Each requires teamwork, **debating**, and **compromising**. First, a senator or representative introduces the idea. The idea can come from many people. It can come from the president, other members of Congress, or regular citizens like you!

When an idea for a law is written down and explained, it is called a **bill**. Next, the bill needs

Representatives talk to people in their community.

Representatives have to be persuasive and willing to compromise.

a **sponsor**. This is someone in Congress who strongly supports the bill. The sponsor introduces the bill to either the Senate or the House.

Next, the bill is assigned to a **committee**. The committee discusses, listens to experts, and makes changes to the bill. Then the committee votes on the bill.

If the committee members agree, the bill goes to the next round of voting. This happens in the Senate or the House. If the bill started in the Senate, the members of the Senate will discuss the bill and vote on it. At this stage, the bill may be changed again.

If the Senate approves the bill, it goes through another round of voting. This time, the bill will be discussed and voted on in the House. At least 218 representatives—a majority—must vote for it to pass. A bill must pass in both the Senate and the House to get to the next step.

Make a Guess!

Not everyone in the United States has access to elected representatives. They might not have access to transportation or the internet. What are some ways elected officials can make their message available to all Americans?

When the president signs a bill, it becomes a law.

After Congress passes the bill, it goes to the president. If the president signs it, the bill becomes a law. However, the president may **veto** the bill. If this happens, Congress can disagree and override the president's veto. This means the bill goes back to Congress for another vote. But this time, at least two-thirds of both the Senate and the House must approve the bill. If this happens, it becomes a law.

Ask Questions!

The news talks about how **politicians** disagree with each other. But they often agree as well. Go online and look at laws that a lot of people supported. What were these laws about? Why do you think politicians agreed?

15

THE LOCAL LEVEL

National laws are important. But so are local laws. The process for making a law that will affect a smaller group of people is different. For example, in a city, there is no Congress. Instead, a group of people such as a city council creates and votes on laws.

Getting involved in local government is easy. Local laws are often more specific to the people living in an area. This means citizens can have an immediate impact.

Understanding how laws are made is important. It shows how people like you can have an impact on everyone around you. Even though you may not be able to vote, you can be an agent of change.

Think!

Your community has its own set of laws. They may be different from national laws. Choose one local law to study. Why do you think this law was made for your community? Who does it affect?

People of every age can make a difference by speaking up for what they believe.

ACTIVITY

Make a change! Laws need a lot of support from many people. Write down an example of a new law you want passed. Show it to your friends and family. What suggestions do they have to make it better? Do you agree with their suggestions?

GLOSSARY

bill (BIL) draft of a law

committee (kuh-MIH-tee) group of legislators who discuss a proposed bill

compromising (KAHM-pruh-mye-zing) being flexible to reach an agreement

debating (dih-BAY-ting) considering reasons for and against an issue

elected (uh-LEK-tuhd) voted into a position

federal (FEH-duh-ruhl) relating to the national level of U.S. government

legislate (LEH-juh-slayt) make laws

politicians (pah-luh-TIH-shuhns) people who run for and hold elected offices

sponsors (SPAHN-suhrs) people who plan and carry out a project or activity

veto (VEE-toh) strike down or go against

FIND OUT MORE

Books
Baxter, Roberta. *The Creation of the U.S. Constitution.* Ann Arbor, MI: Cherry Lake Publishing, 2014.

Bedesky, Baron. *What is a Government?* New York, NY: Crabtree Publishing Co., 2008.

Cheney, Lynne. *We the People.* New York, NY: Simon & Schuster, 2012.

Christelow, Eileen. *Vote!* New York, NY: Clarion Books, 2018.

Taylor-Butler, Christine. *The Congress of the United States.* New York, NY: Scholastic, 2008.

Websites
Ben's Guide to the U.S. Government
https://bensguide.gpo.gov
Let Ben Franklin guide you through the whos and whats of our government.

iCivics
https://icivics.org
Find out how you can be an informed and involved citizen.

INDEX

bills, 9, 10–15
branches of government, 6–7

citizen participation, 7, 9, 10, 13, 18–19, 20
city councils, 17
committees, 12
compromise, 10, 12
Congress
   building and chambers, 5, 6, 7
   lawmaking, 6–15
   structure, 4–6
constituents, 10, 11, 13

debate, 10, 12
democratic participation, 7, 9, 10, 13, 18–19, 20

election campaigns, 16
executive branch, 6, 15

federal lawmaking, 4–15

House of Representatives, 4–9, 10–15

judicial branch, 6

legislative bills, 9, 10–15
legislative branch, 6–7
local lawmaking, 17–18

McConnell, Mitch, 11

Pelosi, Nancy, 9
president, 15

Schumer, Charles, 9
Senate, 4–7, 10–15

three branches of government, 6–7
Trump, Donald, 14

veto power, 15
voting, on bills, 12–13, 15

Waters, Maxine, 9

ABOUT THE AUTHOR

Kevin Winn is a children's book writer and researcher. He focuses on issues of racial justice and educational equity in his work. In 2020, Kevin earned his doctorate in Educational Policy and Evaluation from Arizona State University.